A Time Before Slaughter

12·12·09

For Peter P—

w/ gratitude for

yr early support.

A Time Before
SLAUGHTER

w/ Blessings—

Paul

Paul E. Nelson

Baltimore, Maryland
www.ApprenticeHouse.com

Library of congress cataloging-in-Publication Data
Nelson, Paul E., 1961-
A time before slaughter / Paul E. Nelson. -- 1st ed.
p. cm.
ISBN 978-1-934074-42-8
I. Title.

PS3614.E448T56 2009
811'.6--dc22
2009006727

Printed in the United States of America
First Edition
Cover Design: Kevin Atticks
Cover Art: Will Foulkes (Tsimshian)
Author Photo: Meredith Sedlachek

Published by Apprentice House
The Future of Publishing...Today!

Apprentice House
Communication Department
Loyola University Maryland
4501 N. Charles Street
Baltimore, MD 21210
410.617.5265
www.ApprenticeHouse.com

For Rebecca Rose
and the magic of our
time in Slaughter

"Here is the urban Northwest as it was and as it will be. Read it and weep. And cheer. The poem will take you where the I-5 can't go."
George Bowering
Essayist, Novelist, and Canada's First
Parliamentary Poet Laureate

"Paul Nelson's epic *A Time Before Slaughter* explores the history, mythology, and ecology of a place, a meeting-ground for various cultural interchanges, both good and bad, in the tradition of Charles Olson's *Maximus Poems* or W.C. Williams' *Paterson*, but uniquely his own. It is a pleasure to read—enlightening, serious, funny, and overflowing with life."
Sam Hamill
Poet, Translator, Editor,
and Founder of Copper Canyon Press

"*A Time Before Slaughter* walks with great poetical ability the fine and difficult line between the political and the poetical: a fine line that in most poets leads to the political tract, which shortsells the poetical. Paul Nelson, on the contrary, manages to deal with today's world, and its terrible pitfalls, with an eye on creation and not on cheap lamentation: it results in a book where neither poetry nor nature, nor life or history, are tamed; they are exalted, in all its complex reality, through a sustained poetical state that turns *A Time Before Slaughter* into an authentic work of art."
José Kozer
No buscan reflejarse

"Here's one more big hunk of the American shoulder, as Olson carved his from the North East, Nelson takes his from the Pacific North West. It's beautiful time-space in new words."
Michael McClure
Poet, Playwright, Essayist, Novelist,
and Beat Generation Literary Figure

ACKNOWLEDGEMENTS

Poems have previously appeared in King County Poetry and Art on Buses, *The Argotist, Triplopia*, AmericanSentences.com, *Mute Note Earthward, between sleeps, Golden Handcuffs Review, Big Bridge*, and other publications.

"How The Whales Reached The Sea" (First Version), "The Attack of the Snakes" (First Version) and "Elk Woman and the Flea People" were originally published in *Mythology of Southern Puget Sound*, Ballard/Watson. These stories are part of the public domain. The author's thanks go to the informants, Greg Watson and Arthur Ballard.

Dominism is an erasure of text from *Sexual Peace: Beyond the Dominator Virus* by Michael Sky. Permission to publish this material has been granted by the author.

Letter Thirteen – Plum Stain takes its starter phrase from Andre Breton's *On The Road to San Romano*.

The author wishes to thank the Centrum organization in Port Townsend, Washington for the residency that gave birth to the start of this work, and to another that fostered more work, as well as the Breneman Jaech Foundation for their support, A Gathering of the Tribes and Steve Cannon, as well as many people who helped the process or inspired it, including Joanne Kyger, Ed Sanders, Ed Dorn, Greg Watson, Sam Hamill (for friendship, editing, and his example of one who lives the true poet's life), Amalio Madueño, Patricia Cosgrove and the staff of the White River Valley Museum, Wanda Coleman, Danika Dinsmore, the SPLAB! Living Room attendees, Michael McClure, Allen Ginsberg, José Kozer, Ethelbert Miller, and many others. Other sources include: *Remembered Drums: A History of the Puget Sound Indian Wars* (J.A. Eckrom), *Lushootseed Culture and the Shamanic Odyssey* (J. Miller), *White River Journal: The Story of a Japanese Community in Rural Washington* (S. Flewelling), *Auburn: A Look Down Main Street* (J. Emmons Vine), and *Puget Sound Geography* (T.T. Waterman, V. Hilbert, J. Miller, V. Zahir), *endgame.org* (George Draffan), and *Unequal Protection* (T. Hartmann).

Thanks also to Mark Stumpf, Jody Aliesan, Charlie Potts, Cathryn Vandenbrink, Paul Mallary, David Thomson, Bonnie Hertlien of Mindful Touch Massage, the Institute for Community Leadership, and many other friends, family members, and supporters for their financial support of this and Meredith Sedlachek for love, support, and editing wizardry.

TABLE OF CONTENTS

If communism versus capitalism was the struggle of the 20th Century, then control versus freedom will be the debate of the 21st.

—Lawrence Lessig

A Time Before Slaughter

I

Slaughter is a man
Lt. William Alloway Slaughter, a dependable
man, energetic officer, a crack shot
with a rifle.

Slaughter is a town, founded by
Levi Ballard (he plotted Slaughter)
settled first by Midwesterners
from Illinois and Wisconsin.

Slaughter is a notion, an idea,
a process infected full with the
dominator virus what infects
to this day.

S.U.V. or Ram Charger
tailgating driver
with stoic face.

Slaughter's the sunset, apricot
over West Hill
perennial
and the sky wide
and complex.

Slaughter is Stellar Jay's loud
return in March and memory
of Chief Kanasket
November 25, 1855   there is no
memorial here
for him.

Slaughter is a baptism
in the Christian tradition
of total sobriety
a warning about the changers
and loss of the land.

Slaughter is vapor trails
　　what head toward Grace steeple
　　　　as fog enshrouds West Hill April.

Slaughter in May
　a blizzard of cherry blossoms
　　with each stiff wind
and their pirouette in the wake
　　　　of a speeding car.

Slaughter is Indian Tom
　　and moonlight rescue
　　　　of Johnny King
October 28, 1855　　by canoe
down the Green to the Duwamish
　　until safe with Marines
　　　on the sloop of war Decatur
　　　and soon, Wisconsin.

Slaughter is the sound
of freight train horns to the west
somewhere under the crescent moon,
　　　Nootka roses
　　wide open this side
　　of the June Stuck.

Slaughter is July heron
　　　landing in the river
　　　or standing tall
　　　　hunting fish.

Slaughter is the rush of Stuck through rocks on a rainy August　F r i d a y.

Slaughter is the rush of Stuck through rocks on a rainy August　F r i d a y.

Slaughter is the rush of Stuck through rocks on a rainy August　F r i d a y.

II

Slaughter is Executive Order
9066 and trains full
with Nikkei exiles
and Army escorts
headed to Pinedale (near Fresno)
Friday, May 8, 1942   and more
away on Mother's Day.

A thousand more on May 15 (1,015)
over 2/3rd's (684) American
citizens.

Slaughter continues
while the Slaughter
powers-that-be hosted a dance
for the troops at the VFW.
Men well-fed.
Slaughter is patriotic.

By May 22 the last train left.
Sympathetic neighbors with cookies, cakes
candies and rides.
                    Like we were
going on a real picnic, says Mae
Iseri Yamada. One white girl
wanted to go along.

Mae and Frank Natsuhara returned.
Most didn't.
            The store survived,
most of the land lost, divvied up.
Sold cheap.

Slaughter is the view of cherry trees
one last time
from prison trains bound
for California.

Slaughter is the roar of Stuck
@ sunset on overcast August
Sunday, three ducks
nestled amidst the rocks
of the milky August Stuck,
the prop plane whir
cutting through the August
clear blue morning
sky
while sunlight streams
through yoga windows
Slaughter continues.

III

Slaughter is ʔilalqʷuʔ
now just a school.
ʔilalqʷuʔ,   *Comes Together.*
Bəqəlšuɬ
place where you can see everything
or MUCKLESHOOT.

Bəsqʷədis (Lake Doloff)
a place that has whales.

Stəx̌ʷabš
dwellers
at the place what was
plowed   through.

Plowed   through by whales.
Ask Elk Woman
or the whales themselves.

Whales bailed on Slaughter
plowed their way to the sea
left us Stuck
River in their wake.

Slaughter is Sk̓ʷupabš
and Sbalqʷuʔabš   and Fleas'
house – čutəbalʔtxʷ

Elk's daughter married Flea
(they used to be HUGE!)
Let sleeping Elk women
lie.

Slaughter is Sčakʷšəd
a trail to the water.

Dəx̌k
home to Indian Dan and
a fine spring.

t'ilaq̓ʷac
strawberries at the site
of the Brandon Place

and Sqʷobsti   *water lilies*
at Green River's bend.

Spobalqʷuʔ
for the old channel of the White
now dry.

When the changer transforms
he means business.
Mean business, but Elk Woman's
mother
the Mother of all
can not
be

Slaughter is the rush of Stuck through rocks on a rainy August   F r i d a y

Where Slaughter Begins

The starting point is the self.
Its essence is water.
Ralph Blum

Slaughter begins
comes out of
ice.

White River
(from constant grinding
of boulders
@ the river's source.)

A geologic bruxism
colors the Stuck
today.

Emmons Glacier
on the Northeast side
Tahoma.

White, a river free
chaotic
meander as a river once could.

Slaughter's order.

In the distance
the echo of Elk Woman's belly
laughter.

Elk Woman

Elk Woman save me.
Elk Woman rise up from the grave
and make me whole.
Elk Woman I hear you between
bleats of another freight train horn.
Elk Woman why another sleepless night?
Are you safe from the cold?
Elk Woman undress me, feel the warmth,
are you my angel?
Elk Woman ignore the sleeping woodfrogs.
Elk Woman, one more Guinness and I'm all yours.
I crave your smell.
I am deep in your medicine.
Elk Woman, who is it prolongs the Slaughter?
Elk Woman, explain the appeal of baritone.
Elk Woman constant and ferocious.
Why are you waiting?
Elk Woman can you break me up into
tiny forlorn fractals of man
or archetype
or lost boy wailing
in an unconscious world
longing for touch and invisibility?
Elk Woman dot my eyes.
Elk Woman help me see.
Elk Woman nurture me with your tenderness.
Elk Woman, the son is returning.
Elk Woman, there is snow on the higher hills.
Is it choice or delusion?
Elk Woman where are the beanfields?
Why no salmon in Mill Creek
only a human skull and remnants
of vertebrae? Elk Woman
who stalks these parts?
Who writes these poems?
Elk Woman, we need you.

Come and stop this Slaughter.

HOW THE WHALES REACHED THE SEA (First Version)

A long time ago in the valley between what is now Sumner and Renton Junction was a vast lake; the course of the Puyallup River followed what is now known as Wapato Creek. In the lake there used to be two whales; there they made their home. Upon the point of the hill, northwest of Sumner, now blasted away to give room for the Tacoma highway, there used to stand a huge boulder. To this spot the people would go to get a view of the country above the impenetrable forest. From this point they could see the whales disporting themselves in the lake. One day, however, children from the village noticed the whales acting strangely, and reported the strange actions to their elders. The whales had become tired of their restricted range in the inland lake and were thrashing about and churning the waters mightily in their effort to make their way out. Finally on the fourth day they plowed into the land and forced their way through, opening a way through the plain out to the Sound.

The water followed them down the channel, and thus a new river came into being. We call that River STAX, which means *plowed through.* The Whites call it Stuck River. Most of the water in the lake drained out through the new channel. What used to be the main river now became just a small creek, Wapato Creek (x̌to'ləwa'li, river channel). Where the lake used to be is now a level valley.

The River's Dream

The Slaughter day fades into night and the Stuck
river's dream begins as a silver
shimmer.   She is back to a time of red paint power what
reflects   a less fearful state   the
outline
of
bare
trees
and   a   time   before   blackberries   and
relentless settler prehension.   Time of red paint power   end of
November   when the harvest is in   and her dreams are protected by miles of
fog.

THE ATTACK OF THE SNAKES (First Version)

A young man of the šxʷwababc lived at Kwiluʼt on what is now known as Quartermaster Harbor in the southern part of Vashon Island. Once he sought a wife. To the village of Staq on the White River he came and there he passed many days, but no wife did he find. At last, giving up the search, he returned to his home across the Sound.

Now while on his visit to White River the young man had killed a very handsome garter snake. It so happened that this snake was the son of the chief of the snake people and the snake chief was angry. So the snake chief gathered his people together in council and said: *Let us go to the village of the šxʷwababc and there destroy them; let us make war upon them.*

It was agreed. All of the snake people began the journey. At White Rock near the prairie they came to the bay, near the present site of Des Moines.

Out in the bay they spied a fisherman in a boat. They hailed him and bade him carry them across in his boat. But the boat was too small for so many people. So the fisherman let trail in the water a long rope which was attached to the stern of the canoe, and all the snake people laid hold on the rope until it was full for the entire length, and the boatman towed them across to the place where a cliff overhangs the water.

Early in the morning they approached the young man's village. A lone woman dipping water in a basket espied the attacking party and ran to all the houses crying: *The snake people are coming! They are numerous!* Then the snake people attacked all the people wherever they found them and in whatever manner they could reach them. *Hadeda! ha-ada-a-a-da!* (There is another one), the snakes would cry, as they saw the people in their houses.

Thus they continued till all their enemies were destroyed and they were avenged for the death of the chief's son.

Hops and The Snake People

Slaughter is shelter
from the Southwest Wind
the rain-wind, the
great uncle of Spetsx.

A burnt cedar tree
hollow and charred.
A staging ground.
A home.

A clean-heart
lesson, to mind your own
and be kind.

A snake
on the Interurban Trail
with head bashed in
and 3 skateboarders
on the run.

Slaughter is home
to the snake people.
A place where a snake
's murder   is a case
for war.

Hadada! ha-ada-a-a-da!
is the war cry
of the snake people.

Slaughter is hops
and hops and hops
the memory of hops
and the wealth what hops
bring.

Ezra Meeker,   1866
    got   hops   plants
         planted in Puyallup.
    First in the valley.
Ezra got rich.
         Dick Jeffs got rich.
The Burke House,
the Neely Mansion built
    with hops money.

In 1888 the Slaughter
hops harvest yielded
         792,254 pounds.

First People from
    far as Alaska
         and BC
set up camps in the fields
    and picked
    for a buck a box
       of hops.

No shortage of
entertainment in saloons,
    roulette wheels,
horses race down Main Street.

The valley, dotted
    with hops kilns
       to cure.

BEER A SLAUGHTER CURE?

In 1890, the Slaughter
Malt and Brewing Co:
(A Healthful tone to the Stomach)
    pitched its porter.
A mysterious fire destroyed the brewery.

In 1890, the hop louse
found the hop crop
easy pickin's.

A pesticide of whale oil
and the bark chips of
the South American
quasia tree, used
extensively, could not
kill   the   hop   louse.

The panic of 1893
Slaughtered the hop craze.
Ezra *went to bed wealthy*
and got up the next morning
a pauper.

Slaughter learned big

don't always get

what he wants.

First Jail and Maney Sneatlum

Slaughter, a frontier.
    A frontier
        town.

First city jail built
    within two months
    of incorporation.
        Built
with taxes.
    Taxes from
      saloon licenses.

> Out of respect for the
> Sneatlum Family.
>
> ## No School
> ## Monday
> November 22, 1999
> Funeral services for
> Charmane "Maney" Sneatlum
> will be held at the
> Tribal School
> Monday @
> 10:00a.m.

The first jail was also
    an animal pound.

To this day Slaughter
    gets all this confused.
      Overcrowded jail.
  Humans, like rats, packed
    some shipped
        to Yakima.

Some to heaven.
    Maney Sneatlum.
  Did she suicide?

A city built on saloon
    revenue. Slaughter
city fathers' drunk
    on it.

This as the hop craze
    was ending making
      way for new drugs
        like dairy
and education.

Slaughter is jet noise
  what sends herons flapping
    downstream above the Stuck.

Slaughter is another dog
  trapped inside a fenced
    -in yard, snarling.

A cat up a tree
    not to elude dogs
      but to chase a flock
        of birds.

Stellar Jay
    (a smart man in a time
      before Slaughter).

Stellar Jay, Beaver, and Raven
    slaves of Chinook Wind
      defeated Otter and
          Sapsucker, slaves
  of the cold North Wind.

Slaughter is
    a hole in the sky
      a crafty Eagle.

A crafty Eagle, who
    passes through
      a hole in the sky
  (*a door*) held up by
    timbers at the edge.

Slaughter is men
  doing the grunt work.

Slaughter is sunlight
    streams through yoga
      windows/colors sight purple

silver
turquoise.

The hole in the sky is white
and expanding.

Maney Sneatlum
may be
an Eagle.

Slaughter Tames the River

Steamers on the White River
the highway of its time, before
the railroad.

1871, Captain Brooks Randolph
and *the Comet.*
Langston Ferry, west of Kent
Van Doren's, southwest of
O'Brien.

The Lily famous
steamboat once stranded
a settler Mrs. Traeger.

The boat hit a snag
trapped her and others
Dick Davis, Ernie Brannan.
There (snagtop) they spent the
night, missed
the wedding they were headed to.

The Flood of 1879.
The Flood of 1892.

Periodically, there were terrible floods in the White River area, which caused great hardships to the settlers. The White River in times of flood is a mountain torrent of tremendous power. Gravel and boulders are swept along the bed while the current carries an enormous load of driftwood. Any obstacle which arrests the progress of this drift, fills the channel and forces the water over the banks or compels it to make a new channel. This natural condition operates to increase the destructive action of floods. When water overflows the banks or cuts through the river border, it finds its way through the lower bottom lands. Then it moves down the valleys, seeking a place to get back in the main channel. Generally at these times there are three streams. They are approximately parallel – one the deep, swift current of the river, the others the broad, shallow expanses on either side, moving with less speed. Damage always results at the times of these overflows, but generally quite as many losses arise from the fact that the water stands for weeks and months in low depression after the flood has gone down. As these lands are of great fertility and under high cultivation, overflows are especially destructive. The great floods in this area are usually caused by a combination of heavy rainfall and high temperatures among the snowfields on the western slopes of the Cascades where streams have their source. As a rule, the great floods occur in the fall or early winter. The high temperature acts more readily upon the freshly fallen snow, than upon the heavy packed accumulations of winter. The records show that destructive floods may be expected on the average of some four to six years.

On July 4, 1898 (perhaps)
amidst the celebration
while picnickers enjoyed
(@ Lake Tapps) enjoyed
Independence Day
festivities

EXPLOSION!!!

They done blowd up the river!!!
(Daisy Erickson tells the story.)

A neck of land
BLASTED!
by a King County resident
(they keep his name secret)
BLASTED!
debris
force the river
into its STUCK channel.

In 1899
    Pierce County farmers
      BLASTED! a formidable bluff
          intending the White
to stay in its channel.
It backfired (the plan)
      making the river
                  more
                        Stuck.

It would stay Stuck for a long time.

In the early 1900's
    farmers of BOTH
    counties toting guns
          prowling
      riverside
          guarding.

Bill Hompel, such a
    guard – King Co paid
    ready to shoot Sumner
farmers who dared
    dynamite the
      White.

The river nobody wanted.
No settlers, no changers
    wanted this river.

Temperatures were
    warmer Fall '06.
Rainfall was
    excessive.

On November 14 all
hell loose'd, a
Chinook Wind and steady

warm

rain

steady

warm

rain

steady

warm

rain

directed against the
GLACIERS.
The Flood of 1906.
November 14.

The flood climbed
(the river rose)
2 inches per hour

three   miles   wide

_____   _____   _____

_____   _____   _____

across the valley.
Eighteen to twenty feet deep
as the flood reached
its peak.

No more Northern Pacific
bridge.
Steel pieces of that bridge
took out the county's
wooden bridge.

It took out (the flood)
took out Markwell
Shingle Mill.

Shingles and shingle bolts
careen downstream.

THE   FLOOD   OF   '06.

The J.S. Corbin home
collapsed.
The family escaped
on a raft.

Their barn went out
at night
and not one acre of
topsoil remained
on their twenty acre
farm.

Their orchard
was a mass
of debris.

Bridges   culverts
and Chicago, Milwaukee
and St. Paul Railroad grade
gave way
before the torrent.

People fled their homes

obliged
to swim   or cling
to floating objects.

Whatever improvements had been made on the land were destroyed.

The White (the river nobody
wanted) had a few
improvements
of its own.

This was to be the last time
Slaughter was ever
threatened by flooding
of the White.

Freezing weather
stopped the flood quick
as it started.

The river now flowed
through its Stuck channel.

A flood meeting
@ the Mystic Hall
called by Slaughter
Senator
Knickerbocker.

Lawsuits.

Litigation.

Plotting.

Another flood 1909.

December 24, 1912
the Slaughter Town Council
met
(Christmas Eve!)
voted to take down the
large bridge (once
called Slaughter's beauty
spot)
the old White River Bridge
spanning a 6 year dry channel.

The county offered the
bridge floor lumber
for
sidewalks.

The Game Farm Diversion Dam
1914.
Homes and businesses
in the dry channel, much
of today's downtown
Slaughter.

The Mud Mountain Dam
done in 1949.

Great floods had never been a problem for Indians, who had learned that they should not build permanent homes, which would be washed away.

Old timer Dave Hart says:

*All the poor river was trying to do
was to find the west bluff and
if people would leave it alone,
it would eventually find its
proper channel.*

Slaughter never wanted that river.
He got strip malls
and asphalt riparian zones
instead.

Taming nature.

Ideal fish habitat gone

for

ever.

The White River
met the changers
and the changers
had the last word

so

far

Notice!

Warning!

River Will Be Rising Rapidly
Please Take Safety Precautions

PSE Will Be Performing
Maintenance on the Diversion Damn From

8/2/02 until 8/25/02

The Flows in the White River
On The
Muckleshoot Reservation
Will Increase From Recent Summer Flows
Of About
300 cu. ft. / sec. to about 1200 cu. ft. / sec.

This Will Be About **4 Times**

As Much Water Which Will Be
Similar To Winter Average Flows.
Areas That Are
Normally Dry In The Summer May Be Flooded.

Where Slaughter Got His Velocity

Slaughter's the counterpoint
of rushing flow of the Stuck
and more train horns.

In 1853 the
U.S. Congress
authorized four trans-continental routes
for   exploration.
One, surveyed by Isaac
Stevens, Washington Territory's first
Governor, recommended
Stampede Pass, east
of Slaughter.

In 1860, presidential candidate
Abraham Lincoln spent
$100 Grand
twice as much as
the Little Giant to
buy the Presidency.

Abe railroad lawyer
getting fat from
the Illinois Central, which
got a land grant
with the Little Giant's
support.

Honest Abe gave
more land to railroads
than any other President, land
not his to grant.

In 1862 he signed
the first
Pacific Railway bill.

The Union Pacific/Central Pacific
land grant (amended in '64)
resulted in the
Credit Mobilier
scandal.

U.P. – 11 million acres free,
$27 million
in bonds.

C.P. – 8 million acres free,
$24 million
in bonds.

July 2, 1864, Northern Pacific
land grant.

I see in the near future a crisis approaching that unnerves
me and causes me to tremble for the safety of my country…
Corporations have been enthroned and an era of corruption in
high places will follow, and the money power of the country will
endeavor to prolong its reign by working upon the prejudices of
the people until all wealth is aggregated in a few hands and the
Republic is destroyed.

> – *U.S. President Abraham Lincoln
> on November 21, 1864*

Millions of acres
of the 19th Century
land grants
were not sold to settlers
as the U.S. Congress intended.

Burlington Northern, Burlington Resources, Plum Creek Timber,
Meridian Oil, Catellus, Weyerhauser (Frederick, railroad empire builder
Jim Hill's next door neighbor in St. Paul, began his career deforesting the
pine forests of Wisconsin and Minnesota)

these the corporations
what got the land
intended for
settlers.
Land they rape,
spoil and trade
back to the government
today.

Not the government's land
to grant,
remember.

It became the velocity
of Slaughter.
A changer's dream.

The checkerboard system
and the sell-off of land for revenues
created the shape
of the Muckleshoot Rez.

Northern Pacific chose Tacoma
over Seattle, for the
Western terminus, this
benefited Slaughter.

By 1877, the Seattle and
Walla Walla
started service to Renton
then Slaughter
but soon went bankrupt,
halted service to Slaughter.

Railroads were the Enron of their day.

U.S. 9th Circuit Court Judge Lorenzo Sawyer
perhaps sensing that all things
have sentience ruled

CORPORATIONS ARE PEOPLE

In 1885
Kent farmer Foghorn Green
convened a meeting
with Northern Pacific
representatives.
Service to Slaughter resumed.

When in 1893,
James Hill made Seattle
the terminus of his Great Northern
more settlers discovered
Slaughter in the valley.

An old woman
visiting from back East
on a train from Tacoma to Seattle

heard the brakeman
make the call
of local towns.

Dieringer! (which she heard
as DANGER!)
Stuck! (and she became
more agitated.)
SLAUGHTER! (and she was said
to faint.)

When she came to
and the porter of the
Ohio House Hotel called:
Right this way to the Slaughter House!
she was out again
cold.

By 1895
Slaughter had seven saloons
and 300 residents.

Slaughter had a railroad
and the train-age
state-of-the-art
VELOCITY
to carry out his will.

Slaughter is the glint of summer sunlight
reflecting off the morning Stuck
under the low moan of train horns, always
train horns, inevitable
train horns.

1882 In the San Mateo Railroad Tax Case, U.S. 9th Circuit Court Judge Lorenzo Sawyer declared corporations to be persons; Judge Field was also involved. See the 1886 Santa Clara decision.

1886 In Wabash v. Illinois, the Supreme Court struck down state Granger laws regulating railroad taxes charged to farmers, declaring that interstate commerce could only be regulated by the federal government. In 1886 alone, the Court struck down 230 state laws passed to regulate corporations.

1886 The court does not wish to hear arguments on the question of whether the provision in the Fourteenth Amendment to the Constitution, which forbids a state to deny to any person within its jurisdiction the equal protection of laws, applies to these corporations. We are all of the opinion it does. With that, the U.S. Supreme Court struck down local taxes on railroad property – and declared that corporations were persons; Santa Clara County v. Southern Pacific Railroad, 118 U.S. 394, 396 (1886).

Sixty years later, Justice William O. Douglas stated that there was no history, logic or reason given to support that view.

There were, however, the facts that U.S. Ninth Circuit Court Judge Lorenzo Sawyer was a shareholder in the Central Pacific Railroad, and that he and U.S. Supreme Court Justice Stephen J. Field were close friends of Leland Stratford and other parties involved. Sawyer was uniquely placed to expand the rights and prerogatives of corporations that what is extraordinary is the extent to which Sawyer used unorthodox techniques of statutory interpretation and judicial review in granting the corporation additional powers... [Sawyer's decisions] served as an avenue for the expansion of a corporate construction of economic life, the judicial approval of vast aggregations of wealth and power, and the subordination of the public trust under public utilities.

Of the Fourteenth Amendment cases brought to the Supreme Court between 1890 and 1910, nineteen dealt with the Negro, 288 dealt with corporations.

...for 100 years people have believed that the 1886 case Santa Clara v. Southern Pacific Railroad did in fact include the statement "corporations are persons." But this...was never stated by the court: It was added by the court reporter who wrote the introduction to the decision, called headnotes. As any law student knows, headnotes have no legal standing.

The Snake Chief

Slaughter is a
   crow convention @
      the cedar tree,
  black wings splayed
    in the
     sunlit fog.

Slaughter is a crossroads
    a junction.
  A nexus where people
   of all kinds
     (incl Trains)
    meet.

A Time Before Slaughter
    all were equal.
    Snakes
      People
       Elk.

Snake Chief says humans
    did not spring up
      independent.
The People of the Stuck
    came from Snakes.

They were Snake People.

The first Snake humans
    liked river banks
     and rocks.

It was good habitat.

Snakes were their
            ancient people.
                Never pets.
            Antepasados.

                Wise elders.

These connections
            lost
        due to settler's way.

Swiftwater People
    came from Red-Tail Hawk
        or Owl, some
            big bird of prey.

In A Time Before Slaughter
        Beaver and Wolf
            Deer and Vole
                    Mice and Possum
                Mink and Elk
        were the people who
            lived in what we call
                Slaughter.

Snake Chief says Beaver People
            were fierce
        with spears (a pointed tree?)

Snake Chief says
            these stories
            spark remembrance.

Awaken
            something
                            deep
        in the changers.

Snake Chief liked
to lay on a hot
August rock
by the Stuck
smelling the air after
a succulent meal
of shrew.

ELK WOMAN AND THE FLEA PEOPLE

There is a place on White River known as ȼcutapaʼltxʷw (Flea's House). This was an important Indian village before the whites came. Long ago in mythical times the people who lived there were very dangerous. They were the Flea-people, they say. They used to kill people. They were very large, as big as cougars are.

Elk had a daughter. She grew up and married. She was married to one of the Flea-people they say. She went to live at that village which belonged to the Fleas, on White River. She lived in the big house there; they received her. But they meant to murder her.

When it was the evening, the Flea-people kindled the fire. When it was burning well, they put on a different material instead of the wood they had been burning. They laid on the fire a lot of bones. These bones were green. They made much smoke. The Flea-people intended to smother Elk-woman. That was their way of killing people.

Elk-woman was alone. None of her friends were there. She was among the Fleas, without anyone to help her. She began to realize she had supernatural power. She became angry. She began to breathe in the smoke. Into her lungs she drew it. Deep down in her lungs she swallowed it. She blew it out again. It did her no harm. The Flea-people began to be afraid of her. They saw her breathing in the thick smoke and breathing it out again. She became more and more angry. She seized a stick of wood and began to club the people. She also fought with her teeth. She bit, and fell into a fury. Those Flea-people were soon all killed. Their blood was splattered about.

They were tough people, those Flea-people. The drops of blood came back to life. The Fleas revived but they were small. That is why we have fleas now. If those drops of blood had not come back to life there would be no fleas today. But fleas are small, because only the drops of blood came back to life. If the fleas were as large now as they were before Elk-woman fought them, one flea bite would kill us. We would have blood poison every time a flea bit us.

It was Elk-woman who did that, they say.

Dominism

Power contaminates social
systems   (like) viruses infect
biological systems.
                    A virus   a gene with a coat
wandering
          a spiral   densely packed information
                         (requiring) a   living host cell.

          may *wake*   any moment.   needs
warmth and moisture of
                    (some) host cell to manufacture
    protein coats.
                In   the   end   the   virus
      dominates   while   host cell   maimed or
    destroyed.
                Ability to continuous   and rapidly adapt.
        Pure DNA.   foundation of all organic life.
                                              Thinking
      happens at (this) level. (Remember) no   separation
      between   mind, body and spirit.   Genes know
script
of life   a material universe,
                              responsive to
consciousness   of host.
                          we look for
          building blocks
                        we fight   permanent
                    losing   war.
        Look for   unique
                    field of information.

          Domination   always abusive
    infectious   almost always virally self-
perpetuating.

          The Dominator Virus

passed   through specific interactions
among people.

Moves along   vital connections:
family   physical contacts (especially violence)
sex   emotional interactions   financial
dealings   shared work   professional relationships:
doctor/patient   teacher/student   therapist/client.
Once transmitted   virtual human nature.

We can choose
direction   pattern of relationships.

Infectious   attitudes   and   behaviors within
family systems.

To diminish violence
take serious
evidence   those
invaded
with violence in childhood
continue

wounding   .

Every family reenacts the parable of the tribes.

Babies are born free   .

Thomas Jefferson

and   compatriots can hardly be
blamed for founding yet another dominator culture.
Not quite a police state,   more
incarcerated   per capita than any other developed country;
more violence on   streets of its   capital than many battle zones;
thrive on fighting prohibitionary wars; demands

capital punishment of   poorest citizens with religious zeal
                        eager to jump into armed conflict
     @   slightest provocation.

                                    A tragic waste of

energy.

       Thick is the repressive fog of American denial.

       Can you imagine
               partnership culture?

Slaughter Strikes the Railroads

Slaughter Sun - Thursday, November 5, 1891

Ross Matthews, a ten year old boy attempted to cross the track directly in front of a cable car, on the Madison Street line at Seattle last Friday, but was not quick enough. He fell under the wheels of the car in such a manner that one half of his face was cut off, both legs and his back broken. To make the matter more touching, his mother was a widow, and he her only son. When she saw the mutilated remains, the poor woman nearly went crazy with grief.

1.15.02 –
Counterpoint of Lester Young, Lady Day and the longest train horn ever.

Slaughter is Fancydancers
what make way for
Gandydancers
and their rail and tie
repair work.

The railroad by 1910
firm
in control of Slaughter,
again
it remains
to this day.

Milwaukee Road
Union Pacific
Oregon-Washington Railroad and
Navigation Company
and most of all

The Northern Pacific.

Slaughter became N.P's
western freight terminus

with a HUGE freight yard
roundhouse

and repair yards
south
of downtown, 1912.
Slaughter's population TRIPLES
1910 – 1920, with 180
trains through town
each day
navigating the Slaughter.

Railroad workers have their
own Slaughter neighborhood
Terminal Park.

Slaughter is American
Slaughter is patriotic.

A member of the C.P.S.
King County Council of Defense
Council of Patriotic Service
never mind Mencken
or Samuel Johnson.

In 1917 WWI
and war (to Slaughter)
means business.

Railroads were run
by Uncle Sam, offered
premium wages for
the former boomers.

Slaughter was a
middle class
a standard of living
to get used to.

April, 1920, after
    re-privatization
      and wage cuts

STRIKE!

The first major railroad workers strike
    in history.

Slaughter rail workers
  worked the lines, the yellow
    press called all

COMMUNISTS

(the Wobblies were still
    wobbling.)

U.S. Attorney General
  Harry M. Daughtery said
    these strikers were

COMMUNISTS

who got orders
  directly
    from Moscow.

Slaughter citizens didn't buy it.

City Hall = Strike H.Q.

The N.P. built a
  huge wooden wall around
    the Slaughter yards.

Shacks inside
    housed
      scabs.

The Globe-Republican
in 1922
the only state weekly with
union bug on its
masthead.

Christmas '22 was
tough on
Slaughter people.

The railroad won,
workers caved/accepted
lower wages.

Slaughter saw no
strike violence and lived
on WW vet's
bonus checks
($1,500 per.)

Soon roads. Slaughter's love affair
with asphalt grew.
Slaughter became the
Gateway City.

The march of progress is rapidly obliterating
many of Slaughter's old landmarks.

Sidewalks and water mains
along "A" Street
wiped out
a grove of 33 yr old
maples
planted by hop grower
Matt Connor.

Slaughter's progress wiped out
Lover's Lane.

The great wooden wall
    of Slaughter
      around the yards
   outlived Lover's Lane
        by ten years.

Slaughter is
    the greatly diminished
      stars
   train horns, LOUD

   motor hum of cooler
      behind 76 station
       and bright lights
  what scream all night

      protecting beer.

Slaughter meets Indians

Slaughter
on a Sunday morning dog walk
sees Indians

THAT side the
Stuck River.

He calls out:
How'dja get there?!?

No reply.
Gesture him over.
Perhaps
the Stuck roar.
Perhaps
they choose to
ignore him.
Perhaps
this a place
sacred.

They build their
fire, they
drink from cans
one
takes off
his shirt.

How'd ja get there?!?

Slaughter ponders the
river's navigation
he

does not see the way
@ this bend
below

the FAA tower
the cliffside
condos and houses.

Slaughter leaves hungry
and somewhat
confused.
Slaughter has a
difficult relationship
with mystery.

Not fear
(too fierce)
but it's there
inside, sparked
by a dog bark
or
another engine.

Slaughter arrives @
the parking lot
where
a Suburban's been
busted into.

Someone stole her purse.

You'd think you'd
come out,
have a nice walk…

II

Slaughter
back in his car
determined

first down Dogwood
(too far west) then
down dead-ended
Hemlock.

Finds Gook, Whitey
Assman and TimDog,
drinking Millers.
BIG FIRE, they
tried to show Slaughter
the route across.

Tell him:
*You gotta drinka beer
to stay by the fire.*

Sunday morning dogwalk.
(Perhaps
Slaughter shoulda gone to
church.)

*Why do you throw your cans
in the river?*

*To see if they can make it
to the Pacific*
Gook says.

They watch
two bob
downstream, racing.

Gook/Whitey's
river memory:
Assman does a swandive off Mike's dump.

Corona Extra
12 pack bottles
$12.99

Budweiser
18 pack cans
$10.99

Red Hook
6 packs
$6.99

Icehouse
$11.99
18 pack bottles

Keystone Light 99¢

Olde English
Reg. or Ice
99¢
22 oz.

Letter Thirteen – Plum Stain

Poetry found in the sky
like giant Mars chasing the full ripe plum moon as if in
love – interstellar courting
is how bodies in the heavens demonstrate –
made gravity desirable again
in the August night sky   above the Honda's pounding bass
a silent witness   above the
bed in which dreams of hook shots and fast breaks are kept.

In the Slaughter sky
her makeup perfect   this ripe plum full moon   fallen plums
messed
up sidewalks all over town
sheets of falling unwanted fruit
the Russians learn about Slaughter
sun
rises   plums fall   and Mars ran away with the moon.

Poetry – the desire to kiss eternity
lives to leave a ripe plum stain on the sidewalk of the future
in Slaughter   where
deep wounds open   but don't reveal flesh   deep
woods open   reinvent themselves in an alder moment   to show
                                        Slaughter the way.

6:37AM - 8.13.03
(Phrase taken from Andre Breton –
On the Road to San Romano)

Fish King Fish Kill
(A Special Operation)

Each yr like the rain
            part of the EXPLOSION
                    of pink

                                        plum

blossoms   shaken from
                    tress with each

stiff Spring wind like

EXPLOSION of gold in Scotch Broom May

                                                    they

from gravel RISE.

            Only six returned in 1986
            to seven thousand eighty-eight
                    in '02.

Coho   Chinook   Fish Kings
    triumph over extinction
                    over thousands of miles
                            star-guided

                                    SURGE
        of will over the
                    irrepressible
                            Slaughter.

        THESE thousand silver
                humans got the river
                            pulled out from under them!

    as   for   the   Issei
                    this hard work
            for naught for they end up
                    in slaughter.

To fix the dam
the Army Corps

a   *Special   Operation*
to
lower
the
river

in SPRING!

to fix the dam
water below down 85 % in
Capital S SPRING!

Tribal biologists
survey the scene
of this
Capital S Spring
Special   Operation
small salmon trapped

nearly 1,600   600
were rescued.

In the 24 miles of river affected, thousands of salmon were left high and dry
says Russ Ladley, Puyallup.

I am still shocked by what I saw out there.

Wild Chinook   mostly wild Coho.

The February Stuck
high and mighty
righteous
in its flow west.

The February Stuck

home to prayers
and reverence   liquid path
whales plowed through to
get to sea.

The February Stuck

high and mighty

blew out the diversion dam.

(Kali don't like no dams.)

Quan Yin the water bodhisattva also
capable of righting

the flow.

(This as anarchy grips Ur.)

Puget Sound Energy diverts water
at the dam   through canals
and pipes to Lake Tapps
(once four little natural lakes)
downhill
through a power generator
in Sumner
then back to the Stuck
almighty.

Tuesday, April 8, 2003

the Corps dropped the river
2 inches per hr
from   1,600 cubic-feet-per-second
to 200 on Wednesday.

Fish Kill in the bypass reach.

(A *Special Operation*)

A thousand juvenile fish kings

will never see
the sea
never pull their skin boats there
and back
never return to
(fat and old)
spawn and kinglike die.

A thousand salmon
diverted
below capital S Slaughter

to their own dry hell
below.

Too young to flop and fight
(stuck in little pools of
Stuck River water
stranded.)

Fish Kill   Special Operation   Fish Kill

In the grand scheme of things
this power is in
significant.

In the grand scheme of things
35,000 homes continue
to watch reality

television   on   cable
with
no
idea.

In the grand scheme of things   quote from Roger Thompson, Puget Sound Energy in an April
25, 2003 conversation.

Another Bird Song

May sun river reflection   a perceived bright silver angle with which the
chickadee sings his Thursday A.M. melody going
on bird nerve and the primitive hunger of sound.
The notion of sound as gift   cottonwood down
downed in May on the ground under the dream head pillow so
Stuck in its insistence to follow its plan to mitigate this state we created. A
maple
tree   a perch for early brunch surely this
throat
bobbing bird has a tender
vibrato and a word for Thursday   but until Slaughter relents   it's only nine
cheerful notes.

September's Search for Duende
(After Lorca, For Peter Ludwin)

The search ends when the
duende is encountered as the reason why a bit of bile
is stuck @ the base of the throat   clearly
not
a muse or angel but a
power says Lorca
and
not an angel of protection or a latent antepasado
a lost ancestor to shape
behavior for the preservation of the strain ((the strand))
it
is not madness per se   but
a reason why the ear-slicing madness exists the
struggle what makes it so.   What makes it so deadly
and fierce   the push toward homicide re-directed yet
not a path per se
a notion or
concept concept what triggers the itch no skin-scratching will cure.

It is the fire Artaud knew
burns the cells like a memory of crucifixion
the muscle memory of a spike
blood with no avenue to splurt implodes and marks a soul
like a nuclear tattoo or
powdered
glass in the jar we thot was sugar-filled.
That freshness wholly unknown
it requires a living body as interpreter
exhausts all intellect
that ultimate metallic quality of death
it coulda been an aneurysm   it
rejects measured rhythm   the wild river pours its own path
all the cows stranded on the last patch of higher ground.
The duende is what creates the subtle grimace as
sweet as prolonged uncertain childbirth the
geometry of destruction

one force of nature mother didn't tell you about
has pushed men to madness and Lorca
learned duende scares the muse   it may be
that sound behind you when the forest is on fire
it is the force what compromises your grip on the cliff   a rock
breaks off from under your foot and duende
with the taste of your heart in your throat   duende is
all smiles that you never see   the
styles you break from the moon on a moonless night's incessant tug into
                                        the blood-filled dawn.

Letter 3:05 (In Memoriam Hamed Mowhoush)

The sound of an empire dying's like a torture
field. To break his will brown-skinned in a green sleeping bag
of paramilitary CIA-sponsored claustrophobic
dreams of swarms of birds, thousands and thousands –
has this happened to you – darkening the sky
shorn of all glee – in response to bombing practice
off the record, wrapped in an electrical cord
the idea of a soldier's older brother's torture,
corners cut off all such Geneva Convention pre-911
and laid him on the floor and began to go to work. Again.
What are the voices of dead poets doing in my head
is *beauty the first prod of fear we must live our lives in?*
Left nearly senseless, using fists, a club and a rubber hose.

II

Dead 56 yr old detainee in room 6   ghosts of
poets summoned as witnesses their
voices pierce the edge of the cultural tinnitus
I breathe more shallow at the news I try to avoid.
Have we yet learned to choose *joy over drama,*
heard the news that stays news   rustling
in the undertow of Slaughter near otters in the marshland
my Mayor navigates with new teeth?   Poets are the only ones who cook
                                                                      anymore
head full of voices and ringing ears.   Voices of dead poets
are competing for information overload synapse bandwidth
not resting on this August 3rd for poems, or chicken, or
terrifying news from the latest Abu Ghraib.

His moment came and went and he leaves with a fistful of straws,
shadow growing at 3:30AM, tearing at cuticles with bitter teeth
it will be the only thing that holds back his bile, his destiny
has   all at once
arrived   and he's lost in torture's undertow chasing fragments of his lost
                                                                      faith.

3:34AM – 8.3.05
In Memoriam Hamed Mowhoush (with starter lines from George Bowering)

Letter 4:05 (Multiple Anomalies)

The stars outlandish before the
night of showers of meteors
sky like blurred colors
appears to be fireworks or sealife
and Michael smiles and says *Thank You* and
recoils into a blur of cedar and hummingbirds.

The night is cool in its 3:15 air
stars incline but they do not force your
move back into mayhem
back into a neo-cannibal state
an eye for an eye for an
inch beyond your life outside these bones.

They look at the camera
smile and finish their torture
in patriotic splendor
their unintentional canine wisdom will
own the moment though they disown the
surrounding
dark closing in on them like night.

II

Take the policy official regarding
care
of suicide bombers
the manual now says
little or big – shoot them in the head
ones eyes can never be sure

and Brazilian eyes
they'll go blank on the tube car, they
take a bronze skin suspect with
care, skin color being one
of *multiple anomalies*
you look to extinguish to preserve freedom.

3:30AM – 8.4.05 (From a George Bowering line, from *Kerrisdale Elegies III*)

Slaughter Globe-Republican-Friday, November 3, 1922

JAPS BELLIGERENT,
SAYS LOCAL SAILOR

**Bernard Moran, Returned
From Orient, Says Yellow
Men Dislike America.**

"The citizens of Japan are going about with a chip on their shoulder and are daring Americans to knock it off."

So says Bernard Moran, Slaughter's most widely-travelled young man, who returned late last week for one of his periodic visits after a voyage that took him to the Nipponese Islands among other places.

"The attitude of the Japanese toward this country is amazingly bitter," continued the seafaring boy. "The newspapers print articles that are constructed with the sole purpose of propagating this spirit of disrespect and dislike for things American. The militarists are, of course, doing their best to promote a conflict, and this element is very strong."

Moran brought several newspapers home with him to show the type of propaganda that is being broadcasted throughout Japan to inflame that country against the United States.

Another odd circumstance was noted in Japan by Moran, that being the immense quantity of lum-

ber that is received in that country
from America of which no appar-
ent use is being made. Acres and
acres of cedar posts, imported
from the United States, are to be
seen in Japan, he said, untouched
and with no use being planned
for them. When asked what the
purpose of this importation was
a native replied to Moran:

"When America runs out of tim-
ber, we'll sell all these back to them!"

Slaughter Shikata Ga Nai

Dominism in action   try to
eke out a living near Shira
kawa   busting stumps   working working   hands
bleeding
in Slaughter where
the cherry trees in May still blossom
and the Stuck still flows toward

Kumamoto Prefecture   where the old
ones say: *Dekita koto wa shikata ga nai*
that is: *What has been done can not be helped*
one century of

what's been done can't be helped
all the unmistakable signs of

Slaughter   perennial adolescent
he of Alien Land Law   and
internment of World War II.   He might be
Kent's Representative James Jones   or Miller Freeman of the
Anti-Japanese League   or a prosecutor named Malcolm Douglass
terror of peaceful Nikkei farmers
and reason.   *The*

gentleman's agreement is dropped
and the Slaughter continues with

no respite   exclusion laws gunpoint stickups
and worst of all   when no other recourse,
immolation.   Slaughter shikata ga nai.

Slaughter's Match

Round Midnight
            February 26, 1920
        a dog barks @ an
                            intruder
    no   one   sees.

Round Midnight
            a car speeds off

        the barn is burning.
        The farm is over
        farmers run out
                        with
                buckets of water
        must have dropped them
                when seeing flames
    off high grade cattle

Thomas Christopher's old barn
        now   the Kosai Brothers'
        now   engulfed in flame
        now $15 Thousand dollars
                            of ash.

        GET OUT!

Déjà vu
early Monday January 11, 1926.
        Buichiro (Johnny) Itabashi
        had 74 head of dairy cattle.

This was an investment
                in time
                    in life, raised
        from calves   family   secured

for the night   no match
for the arsonists' hate

GET OUT!

the cows couldn't.

January
clouds tell the story
of souls released
painful lesson of non
attachment
cow smoke fills the Slaughter
sky

GET OUT!

What is the smell of death
meat clouds brown
the Slaughter night

panic in a cow's eye
spreads to fill
the sky above

this particular Slaughter
of hay
and hate

and gasoline
and yellow men who will not learn

GET OUT!

74 cows meet their maker meat their
Slaughter

Sunday evening

@ the Buddhist church
Reverend T. Tsumura
gave the last rites
neighbors advice:

sell the carcasses
of those who merely died
those who weren't
completely immolated

but since   Johnny Itabashi raised
these beings
they who
served him   who were
confined by him
he
discarded that idea
with indignance.

In the days before bulldozers   1926
the Nihonjinkai came out
dug holes
bury the dead
ate a box lunch

and Johnny
rebuilt the barn.

Senryu Sentences

In the days after Pearl Harbor
    the focus of Slaughter
            was cherry trees
    and Nipponese.
       The head of the FBI
         at the time
           was one
     man-loving
       dress-wearing
         large fore-headed

       Queen

    named J. Edgar Hoover
        and soon the trees were chopped
      the internment on.

  Herd 'em up

      pack 'em off
        and give 'em the
     inside room in the badlands
        one columnist said   so
         9066 was signed
    and Tacoma's Mayor Cain
       could not stop it
        and Floyd Oles spoke
       to the Tolan Committee
       Feb 28   and   March 2
            '42.

  Floyd
    his striped tie tucked
      in his clean
       white
        shirt.

His pleated pants
held up
by a white belt

said the huge agribusinesses
in California
resented competition
from small farmer cooperatives.
He got threatening mail
and one nasty phone call
from a California farmer
who spoke all too clearly:

You people have been a pin prick in our back for a long time up there...
and we think now we can get rid of you.

Pinedale
Tule Lake
Minidoka
and Heart Mountain
where soon gardens sprouted
and baths
and baseball games
and dance
and senryu:

I am here, and where is God?
The stars are shining very
bright but it's a very lonely night.

Relocation –
To the east, to the west?
Folded arms.

Now, after two whole years,
Everyone can distinguish
The sound of his own messhall gong.

Sometime between

1942   and   2002
in 60 years the poems
lost their curves:

Sunset falls over West Hill and over where Natsuhara's used to be.

The ghostly disappearing mountain at sunset as the stars come out.

Walking Slaughter streets past the trees whose plums John Napier never ate.

Shimmer of the hot springs pool as reflections of raindrops intersect.

Hooch bottle and Courier Herald box stuck at Green River logjam.

Gook/Whitey's river memory: *Assman does a swandive off Mike's dump.*

So you make the best of it
            it's a diversion
                        you're *good Americans*
            and they got Mat Iseri
                        bearded and all   no
                        toothbrush   no
                              shaving kit

and two days after
            the savior's day
                        12.27.41
            that prison train
                        chugs through Slaughter

            shades drawn
            windows barred.

Jinsei wa asa tsuyu no gotoshi.

Man's life is like the morning dew.

1942
Slaughter seniors
got an early graduation
Superintendent Towne says:

If ever your country needs the
best that we have to offer, it is
in these trying days
but Gordon said:
"No."

He blew the race curfew
turned himself in
Shungo and Mitsu
pleaded
no use.

State Senator Mary Farquharson
peace groups
civil libertarians

but no.
Prisoner of race.

It will be forty years
before the courts figured
Gordon Hirabayashi's right:

RACE IS NOT A CRIME

Vinyl company sign off 512 East says: *Go USA   Melt Sand.*

Canada's flag half mast past the Peace Arch from our friendly fire.

Behind END ISRAEL OCCUPATION rally   kosher hot dog stand.

In charred bus after suicide bomb two corpses in one last embrace.

Almost drowning out traffic noise   starlings in the Monkey Puzzle tree.

3:21P – 10.30.04
Ft. Warden, Port Townsend, WA

Slaughter Pioneer Cemetery

Omura	Omura	Hanson
Scott	Okura	Kashiwagi
Kato	Okura	Teruda
Kometani	Tanabe	Tanabe
Terada	Terada	Terada
Hirose	Hirose	Nishizaki
Yamamoto	Terada	Tanabe
Arima	Omura	Sieh
Sieh	Nishimoto	Nishimoto
Hama	Yamashita	Mukai
Yamashita	Yamashita	Iwai
Takemura	Shimasaki	Natsuhara
Natsuhara	Natsuhara	Natsuhara
Natsuhara	Natsuhara	Isuji
Okura	Faucett	Faucett
Faucett	Boyd	Angeline
Seattle	in	memory
of the	Pioneers	of Slaughter.

Hyundai's and Chevy's
Fly by @ 40
the statue of one who
protects the
dead.
Calligraphy on stones.
Trucks wait @ the
stoplight
by Fred
Meyer and Party City.

The dog waits   the light changes
trucks scatter mid-morning calm.
The KFC is not yet
open. Starbucks is.
SUV SUV New Yorker
with American flag flying
from passenger side   and   the

sign of the fish.

The light changes.   Blue
         Toyota   and   Ford make left
                     turns.   We're all in a hurry.
                       Slaughter rolls on.

The 150 in the left turn
               lane advertises *150 tons*
                         of pure relaxation.
The imploded maple
                     is now a stump   but
               15 others continue
                          the work.

Valley Cyclery.
           Apartment available.
A loud black Bronco.
                         A car horn blows.

Sunny Teriyaki.
            Office Max.
                         Valley Bank.
A white pickup with plates say:
                     GETTNBY

         Minivans and Nissans.
                   More trucks. Quizno's
         Subs.

These are sons and daughters
                   of Pioneers of Slaughter.
                     GETTNBY.

         Slaughter rolls on.
                     The dog still waits.

Elegy for Frank

The train stopped
in Slaughter one
more time last
week.

Frank Natsuhara,
punched ticket,
memory
in doppler rhythm

and

train horns
of
one
last
goodbye.

Another library
now
valley
loam.

How did they save
the store? How
did it feel
prisoner
of race? How
the barbed wire,
humiliation?

Oh Frank Natsuhara
how will they

remember you
in
this
your home
this
big valley?

Plum petals sailing
in a spring gust? Juice

from strawberry

D
R
I
P
P
I
N
g

from chin?

Eclipse Epistle

Did you see the moon honey?
Here on the condemned porch
behind the back door
through evergreens and one
clear October night starred
and miraculous   the Red Sox
lead St. Louis   the air snaps
cold into lungs   I've got
Walt Whitman and critics of William
Carlos Williams and looking at
the lunar eclipse.

It looks more like a moon
on fire   burnt orange and Halloween-
like maybe a part missing
and I could swear coyotes
and children's laughter and voices
from the hostel porch.
They say it's a lunar eclipse
did you see that Wednesday
evening-scale the Cascade star-
laden-sky blue black and immense?

The radio sings slow God Bless
America and I think a lot
about Canada and everywhere there
is fear and the smell of cars
and in the strait seagull babies
pick on seals when they poke
above the little waves that wrap
around the curve of the Port
Townsend beach not far from you
when you wore flowers in your
helmet and looked like Garden head.

Taller, now, in the sky little one
the moon is not as tall as thin
trees this side of the path goes back
into those madrone-lined hills

and paths that cut all the way
down to the strait on one side
and view the sound on the other
by where cannons used to be
aimed at previous threats
to America.

Did you see the moon tonight honey?
I'm writing and reading and
biking and lonely   just like I
want to be and hate to be and
I've spent the last of my money
save a few emergency quarters
on porter and don't even have
cheese and the eclipsed moon is
orange like October   and soon rain
rain rain and coyotes laugh and
howls from the hostel and one lost
moon still higher now and I
wish you could see it black
and orange just like you like
October   before the trees get
all bare   and the air cold and
the rain rain rain   and the look
inside   and the shaking kum nye

kinda scares me in my loneliness
looking for a safe insane way
to explode elusive and threatening
go as far to the brink as I
can without losing my nerve
my hand on the brake   the
tire wobbling and the burnt
orange moon eclipsed   sending
this message to you   like a
hostel voice across the thin
October night air or   better yet
like a coyote howl or laugh
because everyone fears him
and nobody should.

7:55PM -10.27.04PM Fort Warden #256

txʷspaɬx̌ad

Is it a wave crashing
                or the peal of thunder
                            from across the sound?

The field prepared
                the seagulls scattered
                            the waves lap
                                        @ my feet.

Back   back   back   now
                to a time   a place
                        a universe
                                through which a marsh
                                            was drained.

            txʷspaɬx̌ad.
                Not Mill Creek   or
                                Alvord's Slough
                                        or
                0051F.
                            txʷspaɬx̌ad.

From canoes heading out from
                Fleas' House
                            or stəq
        from canoes
                see the hooked toothy
                                    leap
        of Coho. (Silver.)
                        YES   Crow is here
                                Sparrow's morning song
        Hawk on a snag top
                    and still
                        the Heron.

                        YES   Blue Jay is here
                                    Red-winged

Black

bird.
Ann Jack (tawʔ itidolitsa)
                        can see Eagle
           and in her dreams
                    swarms of birds
                            strange birds
                                  spotted wings
                                    purple-

green
                        yellow-billed
     mean
           in flocks
                  to take on Hawks.

   Beaver and Otter   are in this universe.

              Underground Woman
                     and Chinook Wind.

        Raven   the slave of North Wind
           and Woodfrog.
      Woodfrog sings LOUD
              March 2, 1853
                 when
       The Great White Father
            (we know as Millard Fillmore)
       signs the *Organic Act*
             created
           the Territory of Washington.

    Ann Jack   cold hear the Woodfrogs
         loud on the banks of this
             txʷspaɬx̌ad
                 universe.

       In 1890 Starlings were released
       back east

in Central Park.

What were they thinking?

further east a family
named Fiorito dreamed.

There were wars
and blowed up rivers.
There were people
coming like stars.

There this universe of marshland
near Fleas' House
let settlers
have their way.
Sliced up like bread
this land
in tracts.
Dammed   ditched   diverted
square shapes
unknown 'til then
but
in Ann Jack's odd dreams.

Who knew this universe
kept water clean
and Otter happy?

By 1972
the Clean Water Act
and the SAMP of 1990
everyone   but by then
this universe was now
a vast cold steel
aluminum whorl
of warehouses.

Plan 9
would have kept prime   wet   land
in the realm of Ann Jack's
sacred.

Alternative 8
was better
for that slice of
the universe
lovingly known by those
who'd pay a high price for it
as
158260-0065.

Here txʷspaɬx̌ad
could breathe a bit
but Brothers Fiorito
and their Starling companions
got an exemption for a plan
for warehouses.

In 1994 they sold for a million dollars.
In 1999 it sold for $3.3 million dollars.
In 2002 it sold for $20.4 million dollars.
In 2004 warehouses there were almost
all vacant.

But a poem of this universe
would never insinuate.

A poem of this universe
can only remember
the Starling-lined dreams
of Ann Jack.

It took them 60 years to get
from Central Park
to this marshy
universe.

And the Coho still jumps
in a time before Slaughter
and Crow gets fat
on pizza crust
from dumpsters.
And if you look real close
you may see eddies and
Mergansers.

And one warehouse
and parking lot
extending the realm
of Underground Woman
and the dream realm of Ann Jack
and the restless sleep
of nervous bureaucrats
slaves to some hot wind
from the east.

-----Original Message-----

From: ███████████████████████████████████████
███████████████

Sent: Wednesday, April 28, 2004 05:10 PM
To: 'ipipp@scn.org'
Cc: ██
NWS',

██
███████████████████████_SAMP

Paul,

You are welcome.

Now I must make a statement. As a good civil servant I have provided
you with the information you requested. Now that I have sent this
information I will say that I was appalled by your comment yesterday

about the Firorito permit, specifically the implication that since an Italian surname was involved special considerations were given in the issuance of the permit.

As a twenty year employee of the Corps of Engineers I take offense at your insinuation that the Regulatory Branch provided special favors. The integrity of this group is beyond question.

As a second generation Italian American I also take offense at your statement.

I have been advised by my Public Affairs Office that I do not have to dealwith you in future and I chose to exercise that option at this time.

Sincerely,

██████████████

Seattle District Corps of Engineers

-----Original Message-----
From: Paul Nelson [mailto:pen@speakeasy.net]
Sent: Tuesday, April 27, 2004 6:28 PM
To: █████████R NWS
Subject: Re: REG - Mill_Creek_SAMP

S████████R NWS wrote:

Paul,

Here is the link to the Corps Regulatory Branch website with the SAMP documents. Let me know if this is not what you need.
  http://www.nws.usace.army.mil/PublicMenu/Menu.
cfm?sitename=REG
<http://www.nws.usace.army.mil/PublicMenu/Menu.
cfm?sitename=REGandpagename=Mil
l_Creek_SAMP> andpagename=Mill_Creek_SAMP

██████████████

█████████████████
Environmental Resources Section
Seattle District Corps of Engineers
P.O. Box 3755
Seattle, WA 98124-3755

█████████████
FAX █████████████
m██e.army.
mil>
http://www.nws.usace.army.mil/ers/index.html
<http://www.nws.usace.army.mil/ers/index.html>

"To serve man"

<<REG - Mill_Creek_SAMP.url>>

Thank you █████████████

Paul

--
Paul E. Nelson
Founder/Director Global Voices Radio
110 2nd Street S.W. #100
Slaughter, WA 98001-5218
253.735.6328
http://www.globalvoicesradio.org <http://www.globalvoicesradio.org>
http://www.splab.org <http://www.splab.org> - The Northwest
SPokenword LAB
Toll-Free 888.735.6328

Praise To

the river

whose beaches accept
full moon agonized howls

whose grassy banks make
soft nest for November naps

whose rocks have seen a
thousand wailing pilgrims

whose water comes from the
giant sacred Mountain

whose cliffs accept
daily task of welcoming
the dawn.

Praise to the river

whose water the dog
laps up and cools
August heat in

whose course has been
exploded/diverted by
changers in struggle

whose power provides
a worthy model

whose midnight ripples reflect
November moonlight

who demarcates our
home.

Praise to the river

whose course was
plowed by whales

whose soul is
ancient and healing

whose water's the blood
that spawns salmon

and welcomes their annual
star-guided return home.

Praise to the river

whose might is trapped
by Mud Mountain Dam

whose Scotch Broom
mimics the sun
's gold in May

whose berries feed Russians

whose trails seen
a thousand seeking souls

whose rapids provide
the roar restores
the Slaughter
calm.

Praise to the river

who slakes our thirst
without complaint
and reminds us
what it is
to   f l o w.

The End of One Slaughter

The same alder branch
scrapes my hat on my walk home
-Mars can't see through clouds. - 1.16.04

Slaughter
    no longer
        a Great White Cadillac
      more a
    golden yellow hummer
      motor runs
        waits
    in the Winter Summer
     Spring   Fall   night
       sits
          motor runs
    like the mind no
             OFF

     switch
        powers   (mirrors)
         hunger
decimated dxdew?abS sUupabS
suEabS steHabS   left with
    bingo halls   (if lucky)   casinos
 muscle in all
    the wrong places

  humming –
    exhaust perfumes
   (it is perfume to Slaughter)
  perfumes the Slaughter
   sonic train-aided
   Mars hidden
       cool
   January night air.

What might have been a heron

Sam saw *pushing the world*
                                        away

only   a   seagull   south
        he flies   ego
        with   wings.

Humming –
                no start to his
        content
                no depth to his
        conscience
                no life to his
        kiss
                no worries for the
commons
                no control to his mind

Humming -

                only one bullet stops.

Humming -   the black back
                ground noise
                                        of
                sorties
        (white noise)
                        the ring no
        one but he himself hears
ringing –
                Slaughter comes around
        again   with the mask of the
        liberator wolf in
                sheep fur   soft
        but his words all mono
        syllables   modern
                grunts   sharp

humming –

along,   minds MY
business   even tho   no
BECAUSE   I'm   just
a
correspondent   humming.

Slaughter's   a   silhouette
of a bullet in prey
falling
in Fall   in mourning
canoe carried carcass
comfort in a warm fort   so
far
away.
Humming
Slaughter   a   memory
of magnesium   burning
and a life of seconding
that motion.

Slaughter   a mason
quartermaster   commissary
shoulda listened to his father
join the Navy
no
proceeded to California
by way of Cape Horn
seasick all the way 7 mos.
Arriving   finding orders
back to Great Lakes
via Isthmus of Panama
again seasick to arrive
and be sent back West
or so one U.$ Grant
once told the story.

No young officer worth his salt would shun a fight with Injuns.

Glorious rewards

                    writeups in
                    Eastern Press

            but needed dreaded volunteers
                (rabble)   for these
                    thin forces.

November 3rd, 1855   fifty
                regulars and fifty
                        volunteers
            under the command of
                    Slaughter
            camped West of the White
        2 mi so. of its junction
                with the Green
                    a   pair
of woodchoppers   scout   and ten men
        (regulars)   set about felling
            a poplar   a makeshift
                                    bridge.

            Small wars dead anonymous
            woodchopper bullet Indian
            guided in the neck.

Slaughter   a half mile back
        on the rough trail
                to exchange fire
                            bullets

humming –
                over the cold
            White autumn river
                    current.
                Some wounds and near
            misses   bullets   leave holes
                in hats
                        and Corporal Northcraft
                got his boot shot off.

30 dead Indians   their
days estimated Slaughter
and one of them
woman.

Kanasket   Quiemuth   Kitsap
Powhowtish   among 80
warriors   indigenous
who Nelson
reported said White people
were killing only
pieces of clothing
held up on sticks.

November 5   with reinforcements
from Steilacoom   the warm
fort   25 more men
success in crossing the White
tho lost muskets
dunkings
and Slaughter saved
(for now)
missing a swift ride
downstream   - saved by one
out
stretched
arm.
Marching –
across Muckleshoot Prairie
Andrew Burge crossing
the crest of the bluff
this partner in cutting Naches Pass   - spooked

why out from a cedar stump
an Indian BURST
got him in the knee
with slug

Kanasket his bad
ol' self

shooting - saying
(in his own way)
GET OUT!

Flank! God Damn you or you'll all be killed!
the words of one angry
Slaughter   rain

rain

rain

and snow   and no fire
lest they be spotted
these soldiers   collapsed
for the night
on the cold
wet
ground.

Tom Perkins

in his trusty Chinook
jargon:

THE GREAT WHITE FATHER FEELS KINDLY TOWARD
HIS RED CHILDREN!

We will drive you from this ancestral homeland
(they'll buy it with your slot
machine quarters if necessary)
you intruders who
prostituted our women
stole our land
robbed us of our fishing
and hunting grounds.

Perkins sarcastic:
MAYBE YOU COULD SEND THREE WOMEN

and a hail of fire

drove him from the tree.

November 6, 1855
south
of Connell's land claim
by the Carbon River   (or
was this South Prairie Creek?)
Private John Edgar got it
in the lung.   Husband to
Betsy - a Nisqually-Yakima –
this Englishman expired
of gangrene at the warm fort
days later.

Addison Parham   and two privates
of this side-burned
Mennonite-bearded
Lieutenant
wounded
nothing accomplished

paying –
a steep price in
red blood.

Captain Maurice Maloney
called off the pursuit
November 7
back to Military Road
and the march home.

December Slaughter camps
the first through the fourth
three days rest
1855 – the yr of our Lord
by this sluggish Stuck
Camp Morrison – Slaughter orders

December 4ᵗʰ   the march
65 men   - two days rations

marching –
in rain eight
miles of thickets and
swamps
marching –
for glory or the Lord
or to manifest
destiny
or just to die
marching to Brannon's Prairie.

Slaughter with Captain
Christopher Hewitt
and a pair of officers
in the abandoned root house

planning –
a strategy to combat
Nelson's Indians.

Once the jitters ended
Slaughter saw no danger
in fire
to dry clothes   cook food.

Puyallup Tom tried
to warn this
doomed Slaughter
(for the way of Slaughter
's always doomed   all malice has injustice
as its end)
Puyallup Tom saw
the Indian Dog
but Slaughter who
ignored the owl hoots

greeted the soldier
         with the arm load
                  of potatoes
POTATOES!
            for the evening meal
      7PM   and this
Slaughter   a perfect
      silhouette against
         the fire
                  fell dead

   legend says
            without a sound.

   Lieutenant William
               Alloway this
            particular Slaughter

ended with a bullet
            in the heart.

   His corpse
            one of three
      that night
               December 4,
   1855
            the troops marched
north
         amidst the whoops
of jubilant Indians
entering their abandoned
                  camp.

Buried in the cold ground

of the warm Fort
Steilacoom
December 9, 1855
as Masons watched
in fierce
drenching
good
ubiquitous
cleansing
North
wet
rain.

The number, valor and prowess of the Indians has been greatly underrated.

- Captain of the Warship Decatur

Song For Arthur Ballard

Born in Slaughter October
                    18, 1876
          just this side of Ilalqo
               two years after
                    the Presidential order
                         made the place
                              where you can see
                         all over
the Rez.
                    Old Nelson   helped clear
                         his Pop Levi's
                                   property.

Arthur Ballard
                    born in Slaughter
          to be a Transformer
                         knew Latin
                    Greek   Espanol y
                         Esperanto
transformed through breath
                    and whulshootseed.
                                   School teacher
                         Postmaster   Secretary
                                   even City Clerk
                    but his real work
                         Transformer.

To walk up to the place
               where he could see
                    all over
                         and listen.

Listen to Ann Jack
               hear the daylight in graves
                                   listen
               hear the silence of Frog Woman
                         and eat Pheasant with her
                              one good eye   hear
                         the land of the dead

listen

to the sound of one gasping
after nightfall calling
the realm of the dead
where Raven looks back – does not listen
his meat turns to rotten wood
his stench revealed

listen

to the blood comes
out twa' l̓x̌ʷ ulks
west of Sumner
the menstruating rock
don't drink the water - listen!

This Transformer – x̌aʔ – x̌aʔ–

let us draw breath   see
who is stronger

listen

see the belted yellowhammers
the fart that turns men
into crows

listen

to Humpback Boy
complain about
the piece of salmon by
the tail

it's not

deer gristle

listen!

Blanket rock
coulda been a marmot
don't drink the water there – listen!

to she who calls
the Daughter of Thunder
she who sees
through one bad eye
the realm beyond the veil
listen

one child of Slaughter
whose work draws breath
changes worlds

enters a pre-settler time
where up is night
and down daylight
in graves

where Arthur Ballard lives
with the Daughter of Thunder
where people
were not people
but Snake
people
Crow people
plant people   medicine people
people   the day before
people beyond

where bells are not a crime
where land is in common
where shakers sing
where Arthur Ballard
shares bread with Old Nelson.

Listen

and you can hear
the fire in rocks
the blood in trees
the silence
of the time

before Slaughter.

11:19A – 11.04.04 #256 Fort Warden, Port Townsend

Nine Sonnets for Pop & other Poems

Nine Sonnets for Pop

Pop's in the hospital
a slight stroke we figure
but in allopathic terms
expressive aphasia.

Speech difficult to initiate,
non-fluent, labored, and halting.
Deficient intonation, stress patterns
and language reduced to disjointed words

and poor sentence construction.
Sounds like poetry you think
while Josephina arrives from Yakima
trunk full of hand-made corn tortillas.

The heat more than a large can of salsa
can take with the two hour ride over the pass.

2)

Resurrection Hospital where the Sox
could not sweep the Cubs today
adding insult to a speech-addled Father
we've always known as fluent

in his condemnation of all things
like Republicans. *FDR gave me
Social Security and LBJ Medicare
but these assholes* then you try to change

the subject back to baseball.
He was even guarded last year
when the Sox won it all saying
they'll probably get swept in California

when they did the sweeping.
That picture's still my screen saver.

3)

No, you think, their lab experiment
is your father and you know the drill
drugs, surgery or radiation
they're not going to use radiation
Ma says and *don't lecture* and Linda
says *He'll only listen to you* and you
can only say *I've known him longer*
but to see him break down

and cry. We're all gonna die
and death is no failure
but who dies on their own
terms without the Kervorkian

treatment, thank you but no
Jack, I can't hear a click.

4)

There are kids in the lot
cooling off from July
in the early global warming
era, someone has to rescue

the frog, but in Darfur,
death. Plants and animals
are migrating towards the poles
as we set this old spaceship on fire.

Meantime, tortillas, a dip in the Stuck
tender feet don't like the feel of rocks
and Pop breaks down when the tongue
won't cooperate with the brain.

Such perception *The Chinese
will take us over without firing a shot!*

5)

Nations are permanent
as July you want to tell him
but remain silent that he gets it
and no one has to break it down for him.

But the break down of the arteries
and the brain parts that depend on them
means the break down of, not our
patriarch, but Pop nonetheless

crying at the hospital and some
part of that emotionally-blocked
bloodline bubbles up into consciousness
and you'll end up being the last

too smart for I told you so
contending with your own fire.

6)

Too much fire in the liver
the heart, the blood, fire
in that old goat, fire never
replenished as in the way

of the old ones, fire coming back
to bite its master, fire never studied
allowed to lick where it chooses
all the lack of gratitude

fanning that ancient blue flame gone
awry as if you knew how the creator
intended it. Pop, he don't have no
language for it and must settle

for a language older than words
and now all we can do is count tears.

7)

Take a stubborn motherfucker
and hope for grace. Stain
the prayer rug or ply your
spiritual habits down by the river

and maybe the water bodhisattva
has an answer and maybe its
in a tongue you can negotiate
or maybe you just get a gist

or a gust of wind liberates
you from your spit
and you learn to take agony
and be a shop-keeper about it.

Selling enough to keep yourself
in bread, bananas and beer.

8)

All his lessons seem
to come up now, the ones
about what you can get away with
and that you should show up

on time to work. The lesson
of rising early and joining
the union and paying your dues
long into retirement. What

Lech called *Solidarnosc*
how a red flag rises
out of blood but when
the blood is undone by fire

or begins to lose its way
and that eloquent man reduced

to incoherence…

9)

You want to think about his stain
how he had the sense to bring
more fire to a bloodline
and more important, heart.

When his brothers died
when he was not yet ten
he did what he had to do
to survive. And you got that

survival like a lifetime
of clenched teeth and a way
out of wilderness via helicopters
over the canyon and a tuning

of fix that fire into a mode
where somehow there's a *Gracias*
in all of your grief.

8:08P – 7.2.06

Short Train Poem for Pop

No one liked
the black licorice
shipped by the American
Licorice Company

but the red
which is not licorice
yes, I had enough
for the whole class.

Flares were our
4th of July
dynamite, tho Pop
once stole two cherry bombs

the neighbor pissed
but Pop got away with it
this was the lesson
he left, and the train.

And the Slaughter
air it dopples
in the wily
summer night

Ricochets off the West
Hill dawn shuddering
the sun-fed Scotch Broom
in May.

Silver ribbons of sound
veering around plums
preparing to litter
the August ground.

A pause at the Whistle
Stop Cafe, no real

poet seeks to compete
with and

catch an Amtrak
to L.A. or change
taken from the diner car
table   the four year old

(really five) takes
unknowing the concept
of tips, if the Amtrak
is a person

as much as people are
if the horse can be iron
and birth new
velocities of Slaughter

if train horns counterpoint
the Slaughter night
with Lester Young and if what
she said is true:

at the start of every
nightmare waits a train
we've all a train horn
inside us few ever stop to hear.

1:10P - 7.19.05
VSW, Victoria, BC

Tuscan Sonnet Ring

I

Drunk on a New York accent he speaks
not stopping conversation somehow
I had only the pepperoncini
in David's hands, there can be
for he is alive at five hundred
and the sky remains biblical
or cigarette scarred wind
in the tunnel near the Fortezza
though thunder etches the air
above the Tuscan night.
and yet not one Grappa ambulance
or thunder of scooters
when there is no rain
he is alive at five o'clock
no other sculpture after this
I forgot about, but the veins
gulping down the same dish
of Spring Herring chewing on pasta.

II

Too long for a sonnet
we must be content with sex
much sweeter than at home
may be the walking, or the wine
with every meal. Men kissing each other
and a macchiato for the American,
somehow out of step with his
generation and their war. Life
after empire in the land of Dante
we create our own inferno
of teeth-gnashing and affirmation
from without. John Spike
declaims a miracle in wax
and gold leaf what might have been

the sky centuries ago, but
the sky is biblical and Chicago
Blues is a basket with a giant horn
pointing to one lost angel.

III

The blues may invoke an angel
or the general onslaught of fear
we know none such here
but walking Firenze streets
fearless cab drivers, scooterists
vias so narrow, Via Guelfa
operatic Ukrainians in Plaza Repubblica
singing *Summertime* as if forgotten
angels had borrowed her tongue
Summertime into the thick
Tuscan night air accordion music
between ribollita and seared beef
or more tortellini, lasagna
and a life cut out of marble
sling in hand, which David is this?

IV

David a lover or a giant slayer?
David a miracle in stone
and the benefits of a lifetime
of dialogue with light
re-experiencing borders
shaping the spawn of
imaginations ramblings
or lost in a still life
of the public function of the heart
made mute   made in wax and hues
of green   as in a rainforest
canopy reflection in Spring?
An anarchist Spring of no concern
to the cat or the still biblical sky

somehow captured in the hot
glass of another Tuscan memory
shimmering, no, trembling
like that last star on which
we wished for this never to end.

V

This never ends this backward
catapult into the jewels memory
makes from lovers holding hands
shopping for rabbit fur-lined gloves
eating ribollita or vino rojo
within an American song
of Il Duomo and the lost
sculptures of Michelangelo
who saw them there trapped
in marble just as you saw in wax
and black plasma the divine
spawn of your deepest desperation
food for us all. Charlie has your
medicine and if it tastes
as good as the tiramisu
we may never leave. We may
develop a taste for Grappa
and set our bed on fire
high on what Michael called
the drugs of our glands.

VI

Drunk with a New York accent he speaks
of Spring Herring chewing on pasta
not stopping conversation somehow
gulping down the same dish
I had only with the pepperoncini
I forgot about, but the veins
in David's hands, there can be
no other sculpture after this

for he is alive at five hundred
he is alive at five o'clock
and the sky remains biblical
when there is no rain
or cigarette scarred wind
or thunder of scooters
in the tunnel near the Fortezza
and yet not one Grappa ambulance
though thunder etches the air
above the Tuscan night.

VII

An African in New York
adjusting to the Dutch housing
and the energy ripples
insinuating themselves
in glass, or wax, or prayer beads
murmuring their silent plea for peace
or another Tuscan vegetarian meal
how many Euros is that Millicent?
Bill wonders aloud beard biblical
as the sky is again. You
almost expect a swimmer to jump
out at you comparing yourself
to Pollock or the coming of another
Tuscan dusk with a chance of rain
and a Grappa ambulance and an
improbable salad or potatoes
with fur these blatant Americans
and their espresso with milk
and their puny wars and torture
and green rainforest lake paintings
in wax and gold leaf miracles
which might have been the sky
or an Indian Paintbrush Memory
lost on this crowd.

VIII

Too long for a sonnet
much sweeter than at home
with every meal. Men kissing each other
somehow out of step with his
after empire in the land of Dante
of teeth-gnashing and affirmation
declaims a miracle in wax
the sky centuries ago, but
Blues is a basket with a giant horn
pointing to one lost angel.
the sky is biblical and Chicago
and gold leaf what might have been
from without. John Spike
we create our own inferno
generation and their war. Life
and a macchiato for the American,
may be the walking, or the wine
we must be content with sex

IX

The prizes are won
only in the imagination
where we add up the mechanical
Santas and laugh at the folly
of our ardent expectations
forgetting the biblical sky
and the miracle of veins
in marble and alive eyes
a train ride to the Tuscan countryside.
O memory, make me a dancer
to your deepest rhythms
of divinations and ancient
fields of the play of lovers
heating up each other's skin
leaving a stain lovers
a thousand years hence can taste

sweeter than muscato asti
after the last meal
even if Roman gypsies may
steal all the lost tourist's
money. Even if Fred laughs
drunk mouthful of pasta
gulped down with chianti
even if three rings sing
out the essence of an African
experience in New Amsterdam
while we become American
refugees of the blues.

12.17.05 – 2PM

Elegies for Slaughter

Elegies for Slaughter

I

If you were to bitch,
    who among the latent antepasados
        would listen

and if one were to startle
        by visitation, in flesh,
    would the mesh that holds you
                to this surface give,
    would you live for act II
or smash the mirror?

Beauty is the first gasp
    we try to dash from
        with everything a tremble
to recover the flow cottonwood seeds model
           in the late May of afternoon Slaughter.

Every terrible angel blinds us
          with its beauty, each wild pink Stuckside rose
              holds the promise of one last thorn
       Thor knows is pain one day
           protection the next.

The morning trucks growl
      mimic your own desperate hunger
         your blood song gone awry
in the lie of the family nuclear

         and whom besides the cat
      is there in your hour of need
always in search of the edge?

      The memory of Stuckside bluffs
        (where Alice dove and lived)
        is always within the range of a Tuesday

daydream like the last
lost ancestor, inside us like that song we ignore

that we bolt from to muck it all up
with the wrong kind of grease.

Lilac blossoms give way to scotch broom
to wild pink roses, dogwood, cottonwood
and you invent new sneezes,
take a new lover to teach you
how to comb your hair.

If you don't see that flying down,
seeds dreaming of giants
does the event happen?

No. Springtime's an event
sets the table for your senses alone.
The neon sunset colored
arson orange and purple haze
waits all day
for your gaze before it ripens

while Stevie Ray Vaughn's *Riviera Paradise*
elicits 3AM jazz radio memories.

The eagle feather falls
onto your beadless summer hat
only when you halt
your desperate lunges.
Ancient constellations wait
for your cue
to slip into   formation
send off a comet you can see
when the tv's off and your head rests
in your lover's lap.

The green wheel inside your chest
is where the universe

rests its brand of spin

even as a Chinook wind
     tries to tear the skin off your face
   and the race of machines grinds down
      to a certain future of rust
       and blackberries

and we marry a harmony angled
    by Monk and Klook
   unaware the urge to control
  and the jewel in Indra's net
are yet a semitone apart.

II

Allen's voice in my head
        down by the river
    one branch made of skin

one bird drops too easy
        from the cloud-tops
            of this particular Big S
Slaughter.

            and you like an ancestor
    of Levertov want to learn
            the birdsong Yardbird
    couldn't scratch out of a pawned alto.

            And yet the utter loneliness
        a mountain of lost sperm
    slippt through your greasy fingers
    an itch no edge could stop.

The brown hills are muscles
        blossoming out of Tahoma's wild
                        imagination

and we watch every last glacier take Miami.
And they thought they patented Slaughter.

You reached for joy
        settled for drama
                and skin and velocity
        dark   pink   stabs at intimacy
                gropes at your lost innocence

and only dead poets and thunderbeings
            crack the tinittus
                that burns new neural grooves
        when you ordered the poetic equivalent
                of Epistrophy

an ignored neon sunset
closer to your grave.

One, a lover with little ones
behind curtains: *don't peak!*

Two, Czernina who'd spit
rather than swallow, or take
a chaser,   who
didn't even look at the fetus.

Three, lonely, in Charm City
there's a branding for you
teaching the secret
language of lust

and you're unsure what's skin
and what's rust, but know
life of the breathing dead
gets old after a decade
or two.

The rust flakes off
into irises and monkey
puzzle trees, while flecks
of old skin
find their twin, become
parts of constellations that light
the new way home.

III

The guilty river god of the blood
            looks up from the white waves
      of the Stuck to spy
                  an accident carved out of the starfield you called
Aquila

   a thunderbeing's lightning bolt
         carrier whose feather festoons
            the last lust hat you'd burn
      on an island named for an ancient chief.

And time may stop
         but the stars do not, nor the churning
               finite inside lightning
               that begins as black plasma and imagination
   which you in your youth thought infinite.

   The lunge
            the grunt
                  the bolts shot out
      in a primordial white fire/magnesium flash
      delirious juice you only now don't take
            for granted

      like the way your palm stroke
            made her eyes shudder
               or her nails on your summer back
               or her bent before you
               or you her, delirious.

In the night   in the shadow
         below the white of the July starfield
            you wonder if this is the product
            of your own slaughter.

      How many breaths left?
      How many thunderbolts

in your quiver
in your early A.M. tremble?

The rose petals rightly hers
now deferred to a bust
of Kuan Yin

and urges inside are the wars
of the bloodline
the hungry ghosts
or wolves
you haven't yet learned to starve
or feed.

One angel kneeling angel cocksucker wiping it off the chin angel fixing
a south side flat tire angel punching out a bully angel offering a hand for
ash angel witha greasy back door angel who takes it all angel wants to
learn to swallow angel who says no and means it angel feigns an abortion
angel with an endless backscratch angel in the morning in the afternoon
bedroom angel who calls it a nap angel who takes time undressing angel
of undetermined gender angel craves it in five star hotel rooms angel who
makes it go faster angel who needs a nip to elicit the wet reaction angel who
makes sure all the food is different colors who warms the sake who delivers
who's wide open after 5 years who resumes the ancient play of tides and
smells like the sea and craves your scent angel who makes a puddle under
you angel who chokes on it angel makes your feet spin angel who makes you
throw your hat in the fire to combat lust angel with a Cuban cigar and a
wisecrack at any given moment angel who rescues your migrained head with
Canadian cranial sacral hands angel on the telephone angel of email angel
who heals your body from above tough love angel who slaps you angel who
wakes you from your deep psychic slumber angel in pussy fur angel who
dives endlessly from the Stuck bluff angel vegetarian angel who started it all
and has earned her wings and keeps on giving and giving and giving in the
ancient primordial silence who rescues you with a spirit song of your own
making whose ingredients are blood and trust and some kind of unnamable
juju Lorca calls Duende and Yuan Mei calls Xingling and Rilke calls angels
and each tries to put wings and human attributes on a force that lies just
beyond the grasp of poems where glaciers' dreams of muscles become
mountains, verdant stomping grounds for limitless unseen angels.

IV

For an hour
   still learning to navigate Slaughter
      and hear the antepasados' low murmur

  the giant cedar tree's solace -
     a muscle man flext,
        trapped in bark.

     Or discovery of madrones
        how they like to be scratched
          how they, like you, gnarl out
       their own twisted path to the last star.

     Over the centuries the heart
       in your line
         made the wrong kind of muscle.

Let diphtheria slaughter the angels
      you might've called uncles.
        Let the bloodline scatter
  under   excuse of war.

     Let your own personal winter
   stretch on, ignore woodfrogs   daffodils
    lilacs   scotch broom is this not
        the unknown substrate of Slaughter?

Why does drama still
    push out joy for you?
      What's the charm in complexity?

    Remember the masquerade? SAM
      those ancient Igbo masks, why not
        try one on, find resonance
     in different roles don't forget

libations, maybe bombay gin for angels

who underpin this activity.
Maybe you'll begin to see
in the blackness in which all this got started.

Maybe the cat will make
you remember how to play
the need for a little hit
now and then.

And you dear woman?   Sorry
I could not trust my skin. Sorry I trusted
the low murmur of the ancestral urge
more than the lunge into your moist
curves.
Maybe I was afraid
I would disappear

many years after I created an I
that would not be lost to Slaughter,
an I that could survive
for a time.

And still you see signs
backyard kale that bolts
like you do.
Hungry voodoo

springs up and manifests helicopters
in wilderness, wine bottle
weapon memories

and weiss bier-fueled drives
and you survive without a scratch
every time. Did you think

it was YOU all this time?
Was it a would-be sister
one day stopped
kicking, or would-be angels

who know when to give up
      become ghosts
           push the car away
                  from speeding trees?

Each day stars
      are new measured
      according to their relative positions
         the hungry dead doctor sings again,
                  again. Look up

   you see how your new skin fits
      like Marion said her neighbor oak did
      growing from one nut
         didn't slip out your greasy mitt

while stars continue beam
      their ancient rays
         upon the ways of Slaughter.

V

For Amalio Madueño

¿Quién son esos chulos del cielo?
The cross over.
 The take-off.
  A game above the rim.
 ETA showtime
  or the open J for three.

Now when we lose a step
 develop guile, admire
 creativity of the juke
  and deuce
 off the glass.

The gray beard of Bill Russell
 and a memory of Red's cigar
 or Wilt's women,
  all with widowed skin.

Out of our quarrels with others we make
 rhetoric Yeats said, but out
  of those conflicts with ourselves
  Slaughter will never know.

One day she just stopped kicking
 and a fetus dies
  with angel wings or whatever

they're giving 'em these days.
 We wildcraft, bushwhack
 through realms indigenous
  someone back in the bloodline knows

and shows us in that green doctor
  the Scotsman knew about.
 In those 14 foot high sunflowers
 couldn't save your marriage.

Acrobats indeed
    with speed off the dribble
        and a timely pick
           and pop.

Beauty's the first gasp
    we dash from, then the defender's
      nature and you paint
      your hair expectation yellow
      with a side of botox.

    Try to hold off
      the arson orange West Hill
        sunset, no use. June clouds
    can only hold up so long.

    Los chulos del cielo move through them
      burn bright for a time
        hunger for another rainbow
    J in limelight

        pick a fight with nature
      always lose
      but look good doin' it.

We think we know them
    but what we know's
      apparition
        and what's an apparition
    scares us shitless.

Estimados antepasados
    sacar (please) el hambre
      del muchacho en mí, leave

    the old man's hunger, leave
      all the earned gray, favor

the look inside, por favor.

Stave off the divine
　　fist against righteous
　　　　fist after rock rips
　　　　　　twine, it's only June

in Slaughter and the blueberries
　　　　not nearly ripe.

VI

The cedars above
           the base of the cliff
      in the shadow of Tahoma
are that much more impressive
      when the fog lifts
                    in June but June

is still mountain winter
           and winter forever for unlucky
      hikers.

Some will never airport rendezvous
           with seven yr old daughters
      eyes fixed on ancient cedars,
                while f a l l i n g.

One muscular cedar
      a model for you
           in your flight from Slaughter

flexed, three points curled toward
                Jupiter.

In our own weak way
      we hang on
           so concerned with survival

we don't recognize each struggle
           conquered, each shadow bit
      part played

      IS the blossoming
           until we wonder why
those petals are falling
           wonder how the wrinkles
      the gray and how large are
those things yesterday were just
           tiny cedar cones

or little girls waiting for reunion with Daddy.

Fate's bent away from heroes
      sometimes as much as an   out
            stretched   hand
in summer that suddenly becomes winter
     in the shadow of Tahoma.

¡Mi dios me ahorra!
¡No estoy listo para morir!
¡Dejarme por favor
       ver a mi hija
           una más vez!

      We all smile at the flash
         all who began in ecstasy
         all who recognize a real hero
             until winter makes it moot.

    Burn a snip of cedar
        petition antepasados
           but who turns
               back time?

    How soon after
        one large fall
           does a heart stop beating?

  Blossom at her feet
     or in her memory.

    Blossom at the bottom
        of the cliff
           or at the top of the Olympic
     edge, still holding

  foot hold, hand hold, or the view

of evening constellations. Sure, Saturn
in the sky this week

but at one time you held on
to that night swan

and no one hears the little detonations
like no one heard the fog-muffled
cry from the edge of the cliff
where Jeff Graves hiked the Eagle Peak Trail
in the shadow of Tahoma
not trying to become the newest blur
in the oldest constellation
that could have been you.

VII

Only thing wrong with love poems
is that the poem outlasts the love.

And the love poems never return.
And never's not a long time.

And the invisible
calls up to uproot
the springtime of the bloodline.

Oh, so erotic and shapely
enticing
as the parade of Succubi
with whom you still wrestle.

And your hungry inner ghosts dance
with my hungry inner ghosts.
This is as close as they come

striking the appropriate voodoo
bloodline mambo
and your Indian softball
body reminds you
it's not fast
as your mind
no more.

Yet there are highways
for which the yellow stripes
are nebulae

made from the wandering lost syllables
of all those dead poets
whose resonance slip into your dreams
when she's not making plans to suck
the essence from you, one
OH GOD! at a time.

You look over your shoulder
      let dream snow cover your footprints

    maybe Rexroth has some clues, maybe
      your veins can still throb
        and burst with the blossoming

just as you firedance the solstice
      respond to the raised ante of our age
        where everyone's cruel drug
          is velocity.
  And Rosa's red roses
      shedding their blood tint.
        Erun mole.

Turn chicken sausage
    apricots
      y jugo de mango

  into 7 cupped hands of blood
    45 important muscles
    500 fistfuls of flesh
    23 different sizes and shapes of bones
    28 vertebrae
    24 ribs
    32 teeth
    900 ligaments and tendons
    8 lymph nodes
    shit, piss and sweat
    wind, water, earth, fire, metal
    three channels
    six basic shapes of consciousness
    30 daily emails
    typed out in the dry heat
    of Mercury-in-Retrograde
    seven unkind words
    blurted hastily in a weak moment
    and one moment
    where you can stop to watch the clouds

darken, and Saturn emerge

the distant thunderheads are for a moment confused
with the outline of the Olympic Mountains
their gentle prodding

allows the heart-king reign
over all space
and time   is not the wily presence
who steals our mobility, no.

It redefines the heart's architecture
translates for the seeker
una lengua nueva.

This miracle of angels
antepasados latentes
who carry off
wheelbarrow
after wheelbarrow of skulls
from between the legs of the succubus.

But you and I dear reader
we've danced this two-step
eons ago, we

learned this salty mambo
a few poleshifts back.
How's that for 'glistening with creation'?
the canuck said
while chanting his song
to reach that highway between stars.

For they are not as far as we've been told.
They light the sanctum
of cathedrals we've
only dreamed of.

They give the Queen all the fire

she'll ever need.
She who keeps hearing
all those love poems
you keep writing
to other lovers
while she waits, patient
watching the waters
plotting your star
guided return
home.

VIII

For George Bowering

The rez dog looks
with hungry eyes the night
of the first salmon feast

he will eat good tonight
but for him the world's
a feast of big flavored scents.

Beauty is the first gasp we try to dash from
but for Slaughter   sight's
become blindness.

He won't stop for any forehead kiss
lost in the closed of his m.o.
If he did he'd

be lost in that
continuous stream of faces
fish face, first springer face

face of many lovers lost in O face
face of man with bleeding head face
fist through the angry window face
of 6th grade and sliding home safe face
face of the angry man swinging the red wine bottle
face of the governor plotting land swindle
face of Quan Yin forgiving all face of
Ganesh lifting another elephantine
obstacle face

otter face eagle face redtailed hawk face
face of first stellar jay face of mountain
cougar face, snake face, face of lover
on the run, daughter's sleep face or first check face
or straddling Noguchi's Black Sun face
before the setting NW arson orange sun

set

No longer afraid of death
    for the little deaths become easier after
        we dissolve into our hungers
            like the rez dog on feast night, like

        the seagull pecks out the first salmon's
            black eyes on the stuckside beach
                reach eternity without naming it

    settling for the word *be*.
     Study the cat's eyes
          when the magic shoestring
       springs to life again

and the hunter's nerves remain
      kitten-sharp.

You, dear one, in her and her and her
        never stopping to be,
            goal-oriented as the rez dog

with meat on his mind.

                   How you've perfected
       the spectator's glance
           when every now and then
the velocity cools to *manageable*

      no longer a blur
  somehow you see how starlings cohere
      start over the bay
         swerve chaotic in their order
         toward skyscrapers

      festoon the Olympic
        sculpture park
             view

as the last neon orange arson sunset
reflects off Teresita's dream
become real
and you realize

the old you, cracked
can't be patched up.

And children indigenous carry in
the first salmon
under the hunter's
dream song

under an old cloud memory
which mimics your heartbeat.

Sight's become blindness
but some long looks
linger

and until starlings are banished
from Slaughter you track
in your own rez dog hunger
their wild flight home.

IX

Stars are what we are and will return to
after this lucid dream we burn through.

Not yet counting breaths
　　no longer young
　　linger now
　like the May lilac
now coming in April

　　tracking every murmur
only now that lightness
　　has been discovered.

　One shot
　　and then no more.

　No fouling another off, no
　overtime periods, no
　more bleaching away
your footsteps tracking all over

　　the wily paths of Slaughter.
　Then loved ones start dropping
　and you didn't call, lost
　　in your own story of meat.

Lost chasing a bloodline murmur
　you confused with intuition.
　　Who cares now what the score is

　when you start counting breaths
all but the few steps seem like diversion
and the sky no longer pities our fathers.

Take THAT past the next pole shift
　and see if your new language
　　of sneezes punctuated by Stuck

River gurgles makes any more sense.

Or the religion made of dreams
    of Grandfathers thirsting for their lost
star muscles
      replaced by skyscrapers
    and tanker cars filled with flammables
rusty cars in the front yard
      feeding brambles, making
        new fruit. Glass shards
    in the median reflecting light
        from July's Mead Moon.
Candy wrappers in the flower beds
    and gravel lots filled
      with the remnants of explosives.

    They'll never know you walked
      the greasy sidewalks of Slaughter.
        Never know the small neighbor
          favors, won't remember
      your stand on abortion, but festoon

    with flowers
      the tombstones of the scholars
        of war. Your old garden
      will be a strip mall and your essence?

Maybe a poet will discover
    some lost alliteration and write a new book
      on juju. Maybe a son of Abraham

    will plan some wily duende maneuver
      and have an east breeze blow in
        a line right when he needs it

burning with post-romantic bloodfire
    and one of the last of Thor's thunderbolts.

    She said we are the *people*

of the parenthesis
    and the death of the old gods
    plods on

we lose patience for the birth
    of the new.

Moth-eaten English Heather
    we only recognize when it eats
      our overthrown softball
        or scratches our trunk
backing up in haste.

        And what can you show
the angels they ain't seen before? *The dead*
are notoriously hard to please Spicer said, or was it Lorca?
What do the angels want
      besides Indian beads
    on your summer hat, besides
cedar wrapped into a cap Rosa wears
    with a tail of her late son's hair
        hanging from the back?

They demand ceaseless your construction
    of a heart of fire, postcards,
      appetite.
        They demand ceaseless
arson orange sunsets
    and the occasional offering of tobacco
    and spilt blood.

They want to live vicarious
    through your heart-attack-serious
burn   revel in each thrust and mambo

get stuck in your throat in the fetal position
    and force your tongue
      to twist out new sounds
        that chart the heart of

Slaughter's every gimmick
every last dance step.

Track it down.
Get it
on the record.
Tell it slant like the new song
of the old blowed up river.

Or red paint power
underneath a dying sun
or a lost Mead Moon sister
moment

where each of us chooses
Slaughter or plum trees
and the angel smiles
when the first flicker
from that new heart of fire rises
and stays steady in that next
Chinook wind.

X

After summer rain
      angels would trample
           the wet grounds outside
   the carnival of glands
              and yet dead poets
always get the last word.

      Perhaps time sweetens
with each deeply-felt elegy.
          We see their picture
   as if they'd live forever
      the day before the Times
writes their obit.

     It is the rare July
angled rain can eat NW faces, shudder
   what's left of the white blossoms
      who refuse to complain
about their well-timed descent.

   Unlike Slaughter the trees
    the Nootka Rose
      Wild Ginger
        Sitka Columbine
Dogwood, Indian Paintbrush, the Fireweed
     remain neutral, hold

   like Tahoma does
    the resonance of every step
     and waits patient
      for us to honor our greed.

Inside in silence
    except for Friday night car tires
       humming on wet road
   below the sound waves
of earth cutting through space

underneath the dimmest constellation
　　and the sound of the lonely night's last freight train horn
　　　　dead poets pose as angels
　　　　send metaphors for your verse
　　　remind you the whole world's alive
　　　　　inside that green wheel spinning

　　in your chest. Making a mandala
　　　　of spent matches from lit prayer candles
　　　　　and pink rose blossoms offered to the Lady.

　　　　You are only a reflection
　　　　　of a reflection
　　　　of the skill your parents had
　　　　in the lightning flash

that became you and for which you yearn
　　　　　to return
　　　endlessly checking the weather forecast
　　while the Stuck River rolls beyond the spot of diversion.

　　You get a hernia as your marriage falls apart.
　　　Or your nose bleeds for recognition
　　　　but the grace saving you's
　　　　　the extraordinary patience

　　of dead poets.
　　　　　Dead poets in the garden
　　　　　　scaring raccoons.
　　　Dead poets animating the cat's eyes
　　　　　for a moment
　　　　　　moving molecules
　to drop white blossoms for your amusement.

　　Dead poets caught in your throat
　　　in the fetal position
　　　　like latent antepasados
　　　　　turning the last bloodfire burn
　　　into your richest, deepest song.

Sunlight's headed south now
          faster than the cat can comprehend.
                    Makes the tips of Stuck waves
               more white. Animates Coyote's smile.
Lubricates the stunts of Stellar Jays.
                    Keeps light shining on Slaughter
not waiting for better weather.

          And a poet you knew
                    will become that light
          or that latent angel
                    or that force moving molecules
     to amuse your evening walk
               faster than your aging synapses
     can flash across their gap.

He who could live beyond the last parenthesis.
She who could hold fire in her hand.
He who makes better weather for those who honor
                         their ancestral land.
     She who marks the Northwest July sun's
               closing arson orange and apricot rays
                    in skin, bloodfire and melted wax.

She who taps the never-ending flow
          can withstand every
          parlor trick Slaughter
                    could ever conjure
with the rare commitment to every
               blossoming every species
                    has ever known.

                    11:21P – 7.20.07

The future of publishing...today!

Apprentice House is the country's only campus-based, student-staffed book publishing company. Directed by professors and industry professionals, it is a nonprofit activity of the Communication Department at Loyola University Maryland.

Using state-of-the-art technology and an experiential learning model of education, Apprentice House publishes books in untraditional ways. This dual responsibility as publishers and educators creates an unprecedented collaborative environment among faculty and students, while teaching tomorrow's editors, designers, and marketers.

Outside of class, progress on book projects is carried forth by the AH Book Publishing Club, a co-curricular campus organization supported by Loyola University's Office of Student Activities.

Student Project Team for *A Time Before Slaughter*:
    Robert Burns, '08
    Rich Gibson, '08
    Janet Reuter, '08

To learn more about Apprentice House books or to obtain submission guidelines, please visit www.apprenticehouse.com.

Apprentice House
Communication Department
Loyola University Maryland
4501 N. Charles Street
Baltimore, MD 21210
Ph: 410-617-5265
www.ApprenticeHouse.com
info@apprenticehouse.com

Breinigsville, PA USA
20 November 2009
227948BV00001B/2/P